Original title:

Petals and Parables

Copyright © 2025 Creative Arts Management OÜ
All rights reserved.

Author: Julian Montgomery
ISBN HARDBACK: 978-1-80566-687-5
ISBN PAPERBACK: 978-1-80566-972-2

Sonnet of the Sun-drenched Meadow

In a meadow where daisies dance so fine,
A bee buzzed, mistaking a shoe for a shrine.
It landed with pride, giving folks quite a laugh,
As a squirrel rolled by, launching its own photograph.

The sun winked down, as if in on the plot,
While the daisies exchanged secrets, forgetting the hot.
A rabbit took notes on the shenanigans near,
Declaring the meadow a theater of cheer.

Nature's Hidden Dialogues

A butterfly whispered to a sleepy old tree,
'You've got stories of yore, come share one with me!'
The tree creaked softly, a tale to unfold,
Of acorns and shadows, both timid and bold.

A mischievous wind joined, with laughter and spins,
It tickled the leaves, and the gossip begins.
The flowers all giggled, they couldn't contain,
As the daisies shared tales of their joy and pain.

The Blooming Heart's Silhouettes

In the garden of laughter, where colors collide,
The tulips were gossiping with petals wide,
'Have you seen my cousin? She's bloomed as a star!'
Said a daisy with flair, who thought she went far.

The roses chimed in, 'We must have a ball!'
They planned a grand dance, for one and for all.
With twirls and with sways, the night was alive,
When daisies, in frills, tried hard to survive.

Shadows and Stems: A Journey

On a path built of shadows, a stem took a trip,
It stumbled on roots, and began to lose grip.
Willow and oak chuckled, their leaves in a spin,
As the brave little stem sought to conquer and win.

The journey was wobbly, each step one of cheer,
It stopped for a moment, to nibble on fear.
A snail passed by, with a wink and a grin,
'Take it slow, little stem, as the fun's about to begin!'

Lyrics of the Lavender

In a garden full of purple,
The bees dance like they're in a circle.
A squirrel steals lavender for a snack,
But forgets where he hid that pack.

The flowers gossip, oh so sweet,
About the bugs with tiny feet.
A ladybug claims she's got style,
While the snail just grins with a sly smile.

The Blooming Chronicles

Once a tulip thought it was grand,
Sprouting tall, trying to stand.
But a breeze gave it quite a fright,
And down it flopped, oh what a sight!

The daffodils chuckled, having fun,
At a wobbly bloom, just not quite done.
They sip their dew, all bright and cheery,
While the crooked stalk feels a bit weary.

Secrets Beneath the Surface

Underneath the soil so brown,
Worms hold court, wearing crowns upside down.
They debate if they're underground kings,
While a mole hums and dances, sings.

A potato pipes up, all full of starch,
Says, "Life's a treasure, let's all make a march!"
But the carrots just giggle, stuck in their place,
And the onions cry tears that they can't erase.

Serenade of the Sunlit

In the sunlight where the daisies play,
A grasshopper jumps, but goes the wrong way.
He lands on a flower with a funny pop,
And the petals start laughing, they just can't stop!

A butterfly comes, all sparkling bright,
And teases the grasshopper, "You missed the flight!"
They twirl and sway in a floral dance,
As the bees join in, every chance they prance.

Lessons from Nature's Palette

A leaf once tried to skateboard,
It crashed right into a gourd.
The gourd just laughed so loud and clear,
'At least you ride without a fear!'

A flower wore a silly hat,
It swayed and danced, imagine that!
The bees all buzzed a merry tune,
While snails had races 'neath the moon.

A sprout that dreamed of flying high,
Got tangled in a butterfly.
It flapped and flopped with all its might,
And learned that dreams can take a bite.

In gardens filled with jest and cheer,
Each wink and bloom brings laughter near.
So next time life feels like a chore,
Remember, nature's quirks offer more!

Chronicles of the Blooming Heart

A rose once sent a text to spring,
It said, 'Oh joy! Could you take wing?
I'd bloom much brighter with some sun,
But I'm stuck in the shade, it's not much fun!'

A daffodil tried comedy,
It told a joke with glee and spree.
The daisies rolled upon the ground,
While squirrels laughed, both wild and sound.

The lilacs held a talent show,
Each blossom danced, putting on a show.
A humble bud just shyly sang,
And every petal joyfully sprang.

In laughter's wake, the garden thrived,
From morning dew, the joy derived.
With every joke and jape they play,
Nature blooms in the funniest way!

Insights from the Garden's Embrace

In the garden, wisdom flows,
Like daisies pressing on their toes.
A wise old oak would often say,
'Take life lightly, like a play!'

A pumpkin thought it could outgrow,
The apple tree's tall sunlit glow.
But pumpkins knew one secret sure,
They'd roll away—while apples endure!

The violets whispered, 'Aren't we bright?'
But sunflowers boasted, 'We're a sight!'
Yet in their squabble, petals fell,
Creating colors as they quelled.

In nature's arms of laughs and peace,
The simple joy will never cease.
So when in doubt, just tip your hat,
And join the fun; imagine that!

The Tapestry of Green and Gold

A squirrel tried to braid its tail,
But ended up with quite a trail.
With acorns scattered everywhere,
It laughed and claimed it was a hair!

A vine that tangled with a fence,
Declared, 'Oh look! It's purely dense!'
While daisies giggled all around,
'We think your style is truly found!'

The grass blades formed a kickball crew,
And played 'til dusk with skies so blue.
The blooms cheered on each slide and roll,
As laughter filled the garden's soul.

In whispers soft and laughter bold,
This tapestry of green and gold.
Where nature crochets mishaps sweet,
In every stitch, the funny beats!

Fables from the Flora

Once a daisy thought she'd dance,
But tripped on grass and lost her pants!
The ants all laughed, 'Oh what a sight!'
As she blushed red beneath the light.

A rose declared, 'I'm quite the queen!'
While thorns complained, 'You're just too mean.'
Yet in the garden's grand parade,
They pranced together, unafraid.

A tulip said, 'I'm really smart!'
But got confused in playing art.
She painted petals in the sky,
And sparked a laughing butterfly.

The fern just sighed, 'Oh, what a show!'
As flowers giggled, row by row.
In the lush green land where tales ignite,
Laughter blooms from left to right.

The Soft Symphony of Growth

In the sun, the buds did sway,
Complaining loud about their pay.
The daisies hummed a silly tune,
While bees just buzzed to the moon.

A sunflower stretched, feeling grand,
But tripped over a clumsy hand.
'Hey! Mind my leaves, you clumsy bee!'
But laughed despite—'It's funny, see?'

The violets whispered, 'Let's compete!'
In a hopping race with tiny feet.
A ladybug joined, oh what a fling—
'They're all so quick, I'll just take wing!'

In this garden's grand ballet,
Giggles bloom, they frolic and play.
Each twist and turn, a dance on slopes,
Creating joy and wild hopes.

Fragments of Floral Wisdom

The tulip said, 'Don't be so shy,'
While dandelions floated by.
'Embrace the breeze, let laughter flow,'
The petals chimed, 'Just steal the show!'

A wise old rose, with thorns to spare,
Grumbled, 'Watch out—take care, beware!'
But full of joy, she'd roll her eyes,
As everyone laughed at their own ties.

The orchids plotted sneaky schemes,
To steal the sun's warm golden beams.
But ended tangled in each other,
'Who knew we'd play like sister and brother!'

Oh, in the garden's quirky ways,
Floral humor brightens days.
For in the laughter, blooms unfold,
And wisdom's secrets soon retold.

Beneath the Petal's Veil

Beneath the soft and leafy shroud,
A daisy whispered to the crowd.
'What secrets hide beneath our hue?'
'Oh, laughter blooms; it's tried and true!'

The violets giggled, 'Just you wait!'
While marigolds concocted fate.
'Let's hold a contest, who can snicker?'
Each bloom would shine, the blooms were quicker!

Each petal knew a little jest,
That made the garden feel so blessed.
With humor woven in their seams,
They danced along, fulfilling dreams.

So every flower, bright and sweet,
Found joy in life as their own treat.
With every laugh, their colors grew,
A party bloomed that felt so new.

The Dance of the Fragile

In the garden where secrets play,
A daisy dressed in bright array.
It wobbles like a clumsy clown,
And twirls without a hint of frown.

Bumblebees buzz with a cheeky grin,
As petals blush, inviting them in.
They jostle and wrestle in the sun,
'Tis a royal rumble — oh, what fun!

Butterflies flaunt their fancy attire,
Performing stunts, like they're on fire.
Each leap and flap, a wild display,
As they sip sweet nectar on their way.

But when the wind starts to play a tune,
They twirl and spin, oh how they swoon!
The bumblebees chuckle, "Oh, look at them go!"
In this whimsical world where laughter does flow.

Remnants of Spring's Reverie

A crooked bloom with a crinkled leaf,
Sighs of laughter mixed with grief.
It shares its tales of when it was bold,
And how it sparkled like threads of gold.

Petals parade through the gentle breeze,
With stories that tickle like a tease.
One bud claims to have danced with the moon,
While another insists it hummed a tune.

Amidst the jest, a flower trips,
Spreading laughter with each little slip.
"Oh, why so serious?" it giggles with glee,
"In the world of blooms, we must be free!"

As buds exchange their whimsical lore,
The sun dips low, but they want more.
With every tickle the wind drafts anew,
Spring's remnants laugh, as if on cue.

Secrets in the Garden

In whispers, the daisies giggle and sway,
They plot against weeds, come what may.
A garden gnome grins, his secret so sly,
While squirrels hold court, oh me, oh my!

Over the fence, the neighbor's cat naps,
Dreaming of mice and sweet little traps.
The flowers conspire, a raucous brigade,
In a world where the sunflowers serenade!

Elegies of the Fragrant

A rose sighed softly, so sad but sweet,
"I lost my perfume to a clumsy bee's feet."
While lilacs all chuckled, their scent in the air,
"Don't fret little buddy, it's just fate's flair!"

Daffodils danced, dressed bright in gold,
"Your scent's not your worth; just watch us unfold!"
Together they laughed, a bouquet of cheer,
With petals so bright, oh, the fun they endear!

Tales Woven in Silk

The spider spun tales, all round and round,
Of sticky mishaps and insects she found.
A butterfly laughed, "What a web you weave,
With fables so funny, who would believe?"

A moth flitted by, with a wink and a tease,
"Your story's like fabric—full of much ease!"
They shared their tall tales beneath the night sky,
In a world of spun silk, where laughter can fly!

Echoes of Nature's Dialogue

The trees held a meeting, so grand and so wise,
"Did you hear about the squirrel who wears a disguise?"
They roared with laughter, those branches so tall,
As leaves whispered secrets, oh, one and all!

A brook chimed in, a bubbling delight,
"Water your stories, keep them so bright!"
Together they bantered, from dawn to dusk,
In nature's own chat, there's always a bust!

The Blooming Odyssey

In a garden full of chatter,
The gnomes plot with their hats.
A sunflower's got a gossip,
While the daisies roll in spats.

The roses laugh at their thorns,
"Pointy but oh so cute!"
A bee steals nectar for laughs,
Then trips in clover's loot.

Each petal holds a secret,
While worms dance in delight.
A scarecrow sings a ballad,
As the mushrooms join the fight.

With laughter blooming like spring,
Nature's comedy so bright.
Petals flap, bees take wing,
In this garden of pure light.

Legends in Bloom

Once a tulip played the fool,
Telling jokes to a busy bee.
But the bee, quite perplexed,
Buzzed off to find some tea.

A daffodil wore a tutu,
Dancing beneath the sun.
The daisies joined the dance,
And the fun had just begun.

Every stalk has stories,
Fables tucked by the root.
The grass whispers ancient tales,
Of a snail who stole a boot.

When the moon hangs low,
And the stars start to wink,
The garden's laughter echoes,
While the crickets start to think.

Tales from the Thicket

In the thicket, a fox plays tricks,
Swapping hats with the bluebird.
The owl hoots, "Oh the mix!"
While the rabbits cheer and herd.

A toad croaks out a tale,
Of a frog who loves to skate.
With lily pads as his floor,
He pirouettes on fate.

Vines hang like party streamers,
Each twist has a punchline.
The raccoon steals the spotlight,
With a dance that's quite divine.

As dusk falls, the fireflies blink,
Telling secrets in the night.
In the thicket, laughter flows,
With a whimsical delight.

Songs of the Soil

Deep in the earth, where critters play,
Worms compose a funky tune.
The roots keep the rhythm,
While moles dance under the moon.

A dandelion dreams of grandeur,
Wishing on a passing breeze.
While the ants form a conga line,
Having fun with floral tease.

The cabbage rolls with laughter,
As peppers join the beat.
Together they sing of summers,
Making every meal a treat.

When rain drops down like music,
The soil hums a happy song.
In this garden of mirth and cheer,
Every soul finds where they belong.

Verses at Dusk

In the fading light, a bloom starts to dance,
A daisy prances, not missing a chance.
The sun winks at bees in a silly parade,
As ants in tuxedos begin to invade.

Around the rosebush, the snails start to glide,
Their shells are so shiny, they take quite the ride.
The night is a jester with laughter that peals,
While frogs in top hats spin tales with their heels.

The Symphony of Sowing

Sprouts take the stage in a gleeful charade,
With carrots in bowties, quite ready to parade.
The radishes romp, with their cheeks all aglow,
While cucumbers chuckle at the show below.

A squirrel plays maracas, with acorns in tow,
Conducting a concert with a whimsical flow.
The tomatoes join in with a round of good cheer,
While lettuce leaves sway, and the crowd draws near.

Chronicles of Color

A tulip told tales of a rogue little bud,
Who dreamed of a life as a wild, muddy stud.
Bright tigers and violets chuckled at night,
As they planned a story that felt just so right.

The daisies formed teams and they started to cheer,
As colors exploded, filling air with good cheer.
With laughter and wiggles, they danced in delight,
Making friendships that shimmered in newfound light.

The Garden's Whimsy

In the garden of giggles, a cucumber tripped,
While sunflowers boasted and cheerfully quipped.
The peas told bad puns, much to the beans' dread,
As a rabbit in glasses shook his wise head.

A ladybug jester juggled with grace,
While the worms formed a band in a muddy embrace.
With laughter resounding, the garden came life,
In a world where the vegetables held up no strife.

Chronicles of the Cornflowers

In a garden so bright, so merry,
A cornflower danced quite legendary.
It twirled with a bee, what a sight!
Said the bee, 'You're the star of the night!'

Giddy with laughter, they spun round,
While petals rained softly to the ground.
The neighbor's cat watched, full of glee,
Sipping tea on a branch of a tree.

Together they chirped a silly tune,
Under the watchful gaze of the moon.
'What's the secret?' the cat meowed wise,
'Just sprinkle some fun, watch laughter arise!'

So if ever you wander where flowers play,
Listen close to what they say.
For in every bloom and creature's embrace,
Lies a giggle, a song, a splash of grace!

Sonata of the Senses

In fields where scents tease the nose,
Sunflowers sway where the sweet breeze blows.
A rose chuckled, 'What happened to me?'
'A thorny dilemma, don't you agree?'

With laughter, daisies tread lightly,
A foxglove chimed, 'Do it politely!'
Notes of perfume in the air float,
While petals wink on a bumblebee's coat.

Then came a snail, with tales to share,
'Racing is fun, but I'll take my care!'
Amidst the petals, a symphony played,
Nature's laughter in every parade.

So dance to the rhythm of laughter and bloom,
Where nature's antics chase away gloom.
Each note a reminder, so silly and bright,
That joy is a song with no end in sight!

The Poetry of Pollination

A bee on a quest, so busy and spry,
Sipped nectar sweet, as flowers sighed high.
'These blossoms are prime for a banquet,' it buzzed,
'Why is the pollen always so fuzzed?'

With mischief in tow, a wasp joined the ride,
'Come with me now, let's take this in stride!'
They bumped and they jostled, a funny ballet,
Spinning around in a spirited display.

The lilacs laughed as they dropped their petals,
'Watch out for the dogs and their muddy medals!'
An ant held a sign, 'No pests allowed!'
But nature, it seems, was feeling quite proud.

So if you find humor in blossoms and bees,
Join in the laughter, let your heart tease.
For in every buzz, in each pollen parade,
Lies a giggle, a dance, where joy won't fade!

Nature's Narratives

Once in a meadow, stories were spun,
A ladybug spoke of a race that was fun.
'With wings so bright, I zoom past the trees,'
Said a cricket, laughing, 'I'm the king of these!'

They gathered 'round clovers, all eager to hear,
Tales woven thick with magic and cheer.
A squirrel chimed in, 'And I once took a leap,
But landed in mud, oh, not very deep!'

As daisies snickered, bright in the sun,
Tales of their antics just never were done.
Each tale brought a chuckle, a merry old song,
In nature's own book, where all could belong.

So next time you wander near flowers so sweet,
Stop for a moment, let nature's laugh greet.
For funny tales hide in each rustling breeze,
Inviting the world to giggle with ease!

Reflections from the Roots

In the garden of thoughts, where weeds might roam,
A dandelion dreams of a fashionable home.
With socks on its leaves and a hat made of twine,
It lifts up a cheer, saying, "I'm just fine!"

The turnips all gossip, they whisper and pout,
"That flower thinks fancy, but look at its sprout!"
Yet the dandelion laughs, makes a wink with a nod,
"I'm gold in the breeze, while you're stuck in the sod!"

Ephemeral Elegies

A daisy once crafted a crown of pure flair,
But fell off the chair with a twist of the air.
It tumbled and tumbled, in whimsy it spun,
"I'll wear this as armor, I'm ready for fun!"

The roses all giggled, "Oh darling, how vain!"
While peonies snickered, "She's too bright to sustain!"
Yet the daisy stood proud, in the bloom of its day,
"Even wilted, I've style, let them laugh all they may!"

Journeys Through the Jasmine

A jasmine set forth with a dream and a plan,
To travel the world, to dance as she ran.
With a sweetly spun dress and a twirl like a breeze,
She laughed, "First class style, I'll take what I please!"

But the vine said, "Oh dear, you must watch for the bugs!"

While the lilies chimed in, "You'll be groped by the thugs!"
Yet she smiled and replied, "Just let me be free,
For every slow poke's just a flower to me!"

The Fabled Flora

In a land of tall tales where blooms come alive,
A sunflower claimed, "I know how to thrive!"
With stories of rays and the shine of his face,
He flaunted his glow, in the sun's grand embrace.

"I'm much more than seeds, I'm a legend around!"
The daisies just shrugged, "You're still stuck in the ground!"
But he offered a grin, "Dear buds, don't you fret,
For a tale without petals is one we'll regret!"

The Ink of Nature

In gardens bright with colors bold,
A flower whispered tales untold.
It snickered at the bumblebee,
"You think you're fast? Well, wait and see!"

The weeds joined in with laughter loud,
"We're wild and free, we're grass so proud!"
A gnome nearby just shook his head,
"You all should really stay in bed!"

The sun peeked through, a golden grin,
"Who let these jokers out again?"
The vines all giggled, swayed with glee,
"A garden's best when chaos is free!"

And so they played, this motley crew,
With nature's ink, their stories flew.
And every day, with laughter spry,
A new tale bloomed beneath the sky.

Chapters in Cadence

In a quirky nook where critters dwell,
A snail recounted his slow-paced spell.
"Onward I glide, with style so grand,
You won't believe how I rule this land!"

The wise old owl gave a hoot of cheer,
"You travel slow, but your tales are dear!"
The brook chimed in with a giggling flow,
"Fast or slow, just go with the show!"

Beneath the moon, they danced till dawn,
As shadows played on the emerald lawn.
Each critter chimed in with a twist,
"Life's rhythm is one you shouldn't miss!"

Thus they writ their stories in dappled light,
A symphony born from day to night.
With cadence grand, they forged their way,
In nature's book, they'd laugh and play.

Vows of the Vines

Two vines entwined, made promises sweet,
"Together forever, we'll grow and meet!"
One vine quipped, with a playful bind,
"Hope you don't mind my leafy behind!"

A squirrel peeked in, eyes wide with glee,
"You two look cozy—what's your decree?"
"To climb and to twist in the sunniest spots,
Chasing the light, we'll tie all the knots!"

But storms rolled in with a thundering sound,
The vines bickered, swayed to the ground.
"Stop being silly, hold on to me!"
"I can't help it, you're too clingy!"

Yet through the tempest, they found their way,
In every gust, in shadows and play.
With vows unbroken, they danced with the rain,
And laughed at the wild, for love is their gain.

Fragrant Fables

In a meadow ripe with scents so sweet,
A rose recounted her latest feat.
"I tricked the sun into setting late,
So we could bask, it felt just great!"

A daisy chimed in, so proud and spry,
"I dated a wasp, oh my, oh my!"
The tulips gasped, their petals aflame,
"That's quite a buzz, but we feel no shame!"

The daisies giggled, shared each laugh,
As clover searched for a witty half.
"Let's write our stories, spin our yarn,
A book of blooms, in fields we'll charm!"

And thus, they danced in the evening glow,
With fragrant fables that all would know.
Encircled by laughter, this bloom brigade,
Crafting chuckles in every shade.

Scrolls of the Seasons

In springtime's bloom, the rabbits dance,
With floppy ears, they take a chance.
A daisy crown atop their head,
They giggle 'bout the dreams they spread.

Summer's sun brings mischief's chance,
The squirrels chase a wayward glance.
They raid the garden, oh what fun!
And play tag with the old red sun.

Autumn leaves begin to fall,
With pumpkins talking, yes, they're tall!
They boast of pies and chilly air,
While ghosts just yawn without a care.

Winter wraps the world in snow,
The penguins slip—who put that there, though?
They slide around with flapping glee,
Making snow angels, one, two, three!

The Sonnet of Soil

Oh rich and brown, my squishy friend,
With worms that wiggle and twirl and bend.
They dig so deep, they lose their way,
And start a dance beneath the hay.

The turnips wink, the radishes tease,
As ants parade with utmost ease.
They strut around like little kings,
While beetles hum and play with strings.

Potatoes hide in their earthy beds,
With secret whispers, little threads.
They plot to roll upon the floor,
And laugh to hear the kitchen roar.

So if you plant, give soil a cheer,
For all its jokes are loud and clear.
Harvest laughs along with the fruits,
Where cheeky roots wear silly boots!

Threads of the Tapestry

In weavings bright, the colors blend,
Each thread a tale that seems to wend.
With laughter stitched in every seam,
And wild designs that dare to dream.

A spider spins her silken thread,
And tells the flies they should be wed!
"Come dance with me," she sings aloud,
While all the bugs just laugh and crowd.

A tapestry of bright delight,
Where fabric fables take to flight.
The needles gossip, tales reform,
As patterns prance in joyful swarm.

And when it's done, the colors shine,
In crafts of humor, all entwined.
So hang it high and share a grin,
As every thread invites a spin!

Petal-Painted Narratives

A daffodil narrates a tale,
Of bees that buzz and kids that fail.
With petals bright, it claims the sky,
While butterflies just laugh and fly.

The rose complains of thorns so sharp,
While daisies sing a cheerful harp.
They argue who has more allure,
And giggle as the tulips lure.

A tale unfolds in garden plots,
Where sunlight laughs and whispers thoughts.
The geraniums gossip, bold and spry,
And every color waves goodbye.

So in this world where scents and hues,
Create the jest, where laughter brews.
All flowers know their stories bright,
And share a chuckle in the light!

Metaphors in Morning Dew

In the dawn's light, drops dangle like dreams,
They glisten and giggle, or so it seems.
The grass wears jewels, a sparkling crown,
As ants dress in tuxedos, ready for town.

Waking up early is quite the delight,
With breakfast on leaves, a feast in plain sight.
The sun yawns and stretches, a sleepy old cat,
While shadows join in with a playful pat.

Birds gossip in chorus, chirps filled with cheer,
Discussing the latest, oh what a year!
The bugs do the cha-cha, a dance on the lawn,
Under skies that chuckle, as day carries on.

Secrets Held by the Rose

A rose holds secrets tucked tight in its bloom,
Each petal a whisper, a classic cartoon.
It blushes in laughter, a wink for the bees,
Spreading sweet stories upon the soft breeze.

Thorns wear little hats, thinking they're grand,
Guarding the secrets with a prickly hand.
The petals keep chuckling, a rustle of grace,
As scents weave a tale of a floral embrace.

Watch out for the sparrows, they peck and they poke,
Trying to steal gossip like it's some kind of joke.
In the garden's bright stage, it's a comedy show,
Where laughter grows wild, and secrets don't grow slow.

Similes of the Swaying Branches

Branches sway like dancers, a lively ballet,
Shaking their leaves in a wild display.
With wind as the DJ, they twist and they shout,
Bopping to nature's unending flout.

Birds tweet their verses, like poets uncapped,
As squirrels tell stories, their antics unwrapped.
The sunbeams chuckle, tickling the bark,
While shadows do jigs, adding joy to the park.

Each branch an old comic, with tales up its sleeve,
Giggling to itself, it's hard to believe.
As the breeze hums a tune, so merry and bright,
The forest keeps grinning from morning till night.

The Soft Murmurs of Spring

Spring whispers sweet nothings, soft as a sigh,
Like a secret exchange between butterfly and sky.
It snickers with blooms, on each path it weaves,
A laugh shared with daisies, under fluttering leaves.

Raindrops are giggles, dropped from above,
Tickling the earth with a gentle shove.
The sun plays peekaboo, day after day,
While clouds share a chuckle, in their frothy ballet.

Grass sprouts with glee, a green sneaky sprout,
Daring the daisies to dance, no doubt.
In this whimsical waltz, joy's the supreme king,
Here's to the fun found in the joys of spring!

The Story of the Seasons

Winter sneezed and shook the trees,
Spring laughed hard and scuffed her knees.
Summer strutted in the sun,
While autumn danced, and told a pun.

Snowflakes giggled, clouds on cue,
Blossoms bounced, with skies so blue.
Heatwaves played a cheeky game,
While leaves exchanged their leafy fame.

Frosty breath and ice cream cones,
Jokes on squirrels, and silly tones.
Nature's jesters in a brawl,
Seasons chuckled, fun for all!

So grab your coat or grab your hat,
Join the fun, imagine that!
For every tick of nature's clock,
Is just a chance to laugh and mock.

Whispers in the Woods

In the woods, a squirrel spoke,
To a tree, he shared a joke.
The owl hooted in delight,
While rabbits danced the moonlit night.

Leaves rustled with a playful tease,
As critters gathered 'neath the trees.
A fox told tales of grand escapades,
While hedgehogs rolled in leafy glades.

A wise old owl said, "What a hoot!"
As raccoons wore their best-foot suit.
They played charades beneath the stars,
With laughter echoing 'round the bars.

So in those woods, a mirthful cheer,
Where every creature sheds a tear.
Of joyful times and shared delight,
These whispers make the world feel right.

Murmurs of the Monsoon

Raindrops tapped a snazzy beat,
On rooftops, they danced, couldn't be beat.
Puddles formed playful little lakes,
As frogs croaked out their silly fakes.

Clouds rolled in, a fluffy crew,
Spilling laughter, just like dew.
Lightning flashed in a playful way,
As thunder chuckled 'Come out and play!'

Umbrellas spun like tops on streets,
Wet socks turned into swampy feats.
Every drip held a giggle's tune,
While kids splashed under the monsoon.

So let it rain and let it pour,
Each drop brings smiles, and opens doors.
For in every storm, there's fun to find,
When nature's whims are oh so kind.

The Dance of the Daisies

Daisies twirled on tipsy stems,
While bumblebees sang happy hymns.
In fields so wide, they laughed and spun,
Chasing shadows, oh what fun!

The sun peeked in, with a winking eye,
As daisies waved and birds flew high.
Butterflies joined in the play,
Turning gardens into a cabaret.

A breeze blew in with a cheeky grin,
Tickling petals, where joy begins.
With every sway, they made a scene,
Nature's laughter, vibrant and green.

So when you stroll through fields of cheer,
Remember the giggles buzzing near.
Dancing daisies know the way,
To brighten up a cloudy day!

The Ballad of Blossoms

In a garden where daisies joke,
Lilies laugh until they choke.
Sunflowers strut in a silly dance,
While roses prattle, not leaving a chance.

A gnome trips over a sleepy bee,
He mumbles, 'I thought it was just me!'
Dandelions giggle, their fluff in the air,
As they plot to tickle the gardener's hair.

The tulips gossip in colors bright,
'Who wore what to the garden's night?'
A sunflower's crown tilts just right,
While pansies paint the scene in delight.

In the midst of this floral spree,
A worm shouts, 'Don't forget about me!'
With roots in the soil, he takes a stand,
Claiming the best jokes in the land!

Echoes of Enchantment

Under the moon, fairy lights twinkle,
Blushing blooms share a cheeky crinkle.
Petunias tease a shy little sprout,
'Laugh, dear bud! It's what life's about!'

A butterfly dons a quirky hat,
Making everyone stop and chat.
The bees insist they know best,
As they hold a honey-dripping fest.

Giggling violets form a crew,
Planning pranks with morning dew.
They swap places and play hide-and-seek,
While pansies offer tips that are quite unique.

With petals bright, the laughter unfolds,
In this garden of stories yet untold.
Magic swirls atop the breeze,
Whisking away worries with teasing ease.

Whispers of the Wind

A gust of breeze sings a funny tune,
Tickling the leaves like a silly buffoon.
The willow sways, a soft dancer,
Twisting her branches like a night prancer.

Clouds poke fun at the sun's bright rays,
'You think you're hot? Just count the days!'
A squirrel giggles at the wise old oak,
'You're just a statue with no real poke!'

The daisies shout, 'Look, it's a plane!'
As petals float down like soft rain.
In this breezy, whispered delight,
Every chuckle fuels the night.

As stars become the garden's friends,
They twinkle with mischief that never ends.
Nature's humor in every bloom,
Filling the air with laughter's perfume.

The Art of Growth

In a pot too small, a cactus sighed,
'I'm meant for deserts, not tucked inside!'
A sprout nearby said, 'Chill out, dude,
You still look great, sporting that green mood!'

Bamboo stretches, 'I'm so tall, see?
But you flowers bloom, just wait for me!'
While petals flutter and roots dig deep,
They share stories they can hardly keep.

A seedling shimmies with ambition bright,
Saying, 'I'll grow and dazzle the night!'
The weeds roll their eyes, 'Take it easy, friend,
Life's not a race; it's just a blend!'

With every sprout, a potful of glee,
Reminding us how fun growing can be.
From blossoms to laughs, it's all a show,
In the grand garden where dreams still grow.

Chronicles of Chlorophyll

In a garden filled with green,
The leaves held secrets, quite unseen.
A sunflower danced on a breeze,
While daisies giggled with such ease.

Bees wore jackets made of fluff,
Claiming nectar's way was rough.
But when the pollen came in sight,
They buzzed around like kids in flight.

The tomato plants formed a band,
With carrots playing in the sand.
And lettuce wore a leafy hat,
Saying, 'Why are we friends with that?'

So gather 'round, and lend an ear,
To tales of plants, both far and near.
For in their world, a joke's no myth,
Just laughter shared with every whiff.

Whispers of Blossoms

In a patch where flowers hid,
A rose confessed she lost her lid.
'What shall I do?' she cried with glee,
'I've never felt so free, you see!'

The tulip chuckled, holding tight,
'If you find it, call me tonight!'
And all the daisies chimed along,
Singing loudly their silly song.

The pansies wore a zany grin,
Saying, 'We'll help you look within!'
They searched behind the bumble bees,
And tickled stems with gentle tease.

While petunias shared a joke so fine,
About a vine who crossed the line.
In whispers soft, the flowers spun,
Their giggles danced, and oh what fun!

The Language of Flowers

On the petals, letters twirled,
As butterflies in laughter swirled.
'Roses mean love,' one flower said,
'I meant to write, but now I'm wed!'

The gardener shrieked, 'What's this chaos?'
As he tripped over a bright eos.
Daisy decoded all the buzz,
Saying, 'Love's the best kind of fuzz!'

Orchids winked in violet flaunt,
While lilacs held a purple jaunt.
Yet violets sighed with quiet dreams,
Wishing for life beyond their beams.

So gather blooms with quirks so grand,
In each petal, jokes take a stand.
Watch as flowers weave and bend,
Creating tales that twist and blend!

Stories Beneath the Bloom

Underneath the leafy crown,
A worm told tales of silliness brown.
He wriggled and jiggled with delight,
Saying, 'I dance when I smell good light!'

A ladybug, so red and bright,
Joined in, saying, 'What a sight!'
She flew around with stories locked,
Of daring hunts and being shocked!

Grasshoppers chirped in rhythmic rhyme,
'We dance and play, just wasting time!'
And daisies smiled, their heads held high,
While clouds rolled in, oh my, oh my!

So listen close and read between,
The quirky tales of the unseen.
For in each leaf, there's laughter spun,
A garden's joy is never done!

Insights from the Earth's Cradle

A worm wore a hat, quite absurd,
He danced with the ants, not a word.
The flowers giggled, what a sight,
As the sun blinked his beams, feeling bright.

A frog croaked jokes, to everyone's glee,
While bees buzzed along, sipping sweet tea.
A cloud in the sky had a snazzy grin,
As raindrops danced down, let the fun begin!

Reflections on Nature's Canvas

A squirrel donned shades, just so chic,
He skated on leaves, a nutty streak.
The brook chuckled softly, smooth and clear,
As it whispered secrets only trees hear.

The owl perched high, with glasses so thick,
Told tall tales of shadows and tricks.
And the spider spun webs, the grandest of art,
Caught in their laughter, we all play a part.

The Silent Teachings of the Wild

In the thicket, a hedgehog with flair,
Wore a spiky crown, without a care.
He taught the young fox how to prance,
While the daisies swayed in a merry dance.

A chameleon winked, changing hues,
As butterflies giggled, mischief in news.
The wise old tree shook its bark with pride,
As nature's jesters danced side by side.

Harvests of Hope and Light

A scarecrow dreamed of strolling the fair,
Imagined he'd dance with wild prancing air.
While pumpkins grinned, quite round and bright,
They shared the best jokes in soft moonlight.

The cornfield rustled, secrets to share,
With crickets reciting poetry rare.
And the sun set low, painting the night,
With laughter that glimmered, a pure delight.

The Garden's Chronicles

In the garden, gnomes take a stroll,
Wearing hats that are comically whole.
Tulips giggle, daffodils dance,
While carrots plot their veggie romance.

Butterflies flutter, chasing a bee,
"You can't catch me!" they shout with glee.
The radishes whisper, all in a row,
"What's a garden without a good show?"

A snail slides by, slow as can be,
"Why rush?" it says, "Just look at me!"
A worm winks and digs underground,
Raccoons laugh at the chaos they've found.

So here in the garden, laughter takes root,
With veggies dressed in whimsical suit.
Under the sun, life twists and twirls,
Nature's antics—oh how it unfurls!

Murmurs of the Meadow

In the meadow, a cow starts to sing,
With a voice that makes the daisies take wing.
A butterfly sighs, wearing a frown,
"Why's he mooing? He's no queen nor clown!"

The grasshoppers hop, bringing their band,
Playing tunes that are surprisingly grand.
A rabbit jokes, "I'll race you, I swear!"
But foxes just laugh, without a care.

Clouds float by, in shapes quite absurd,
One looks like broccoli, isn't that weird?
A breeze turns the daisies into a show,
As laughter tumbles to and fro.

The sun sets low, painting skies bright,
With giggles and whispers lingering in light.
In the meadow, mischief is mild,
Every creature, a funny, carefree child!

Chronicles of the Changing

Leaves start to yell, 'Look at us change!'
In colors so bright, it's rather strange.
A squirrel's lost in its acorn stash,
While other trees giggle and gasp.

Frogs in the pond start to croak a tune,
"Fall's here, best get cozy, you goons!"
The winds start to dance, swirling the leaves,
As pumpkins pop up, like trick-or-treat thieves.

A raccoon, with flair, wears a scarf quite bold,
Pretending it's winter in weather still gold.
The sun playfully sets, throwing gold in a haze,
While nature cracks jokes in a riotous daze.

So here's to the seasons and all of their fun,
Where laughter goes wild under brightening sun.
As change flops and flutters from tree to tree,
Nature giggles, "Look at me! Look at me!"

Harmonies of the Harvest

In the fields, corn dances in lines,
Barley grins, with sweet, silly signs.
Pumpkins parade in a quirky affair,
While scarecrows strike poses with flair.

The sun beats down, giving all a glow,
As ants march in lines, singing their show.
Tomatoes blush as they bask in the light,
Saying, "We're ripe! What a glorious sight!"

A potato delayed, saying, "Not quite!"
"I'm still dreaming of fresh-baked delight!"
The veggies chuckle as they play in the breeze,
While farmers just giggle, feeling the tease.

As dusk rolls in, with stars all aglow,
Nature's concert brings laughter, you know?
So raise up a glass, let the humor flow,
In the harvest of mirth, we all steal the show!

Tales from the Garden

In the garden where daisies dance,
A rabbit wears socks, what a strange chance!
He hops with a hat, so very profound,
Chasing the butterflies twirling around.

The carrots gossip with each other bold,
While the radishes whisper secrets untold.
One said, 'Did you see the snail's new shoes?'
The garden's a circus, with laughter and blues.

A gnome made of ceramic spun in a twirl,
Announcing the plants with a loud, silly whirl.
He slipped on the dew, fell flat on his face,
The sunflowers chuckled, 'What a fine grace!'

Now every flower wears a whimsical hat,
As the bees buzz along, fancying that.
In this quirky patch, joy boldly takes flight,
With giggles and grins from morning till night.

Secrets of the Sylvan

In the woods where the squirrels all plot and scheme,
A tree grew arms that could reach and dream.
He tickled the branches, sent leaves spinning round,
While the mushrooms giggled beneath the soft mound.

The fox, with a flair, wore a scarf rather bright,
Claimed it was fashion for woodland delight.
As owls rolled their eyes at his dapper display,
They wondered if he'd strut in the light of the day.

The brook babbled nonsense, stories absurd,
Of fish that wore glasses and chickens that stirred.
It chuckled and chortled, a musical quack,
While the frogs formed a choir, all dressed in black.

An acorn once dreamed to be wise like a tree,
He burst into laughter, 'Oh, that's just not me!'
So he rolled down the hill, in pursuit of a wish,
And landed in soup — just a nutty old swish!

Cries of the Blossoms

The tulips held court with a royal decree,
'No one leaves the garden till funny as we!'
Then a poppy burst out with a joke on the breeze,
'The roses are blushing, oh, can you believe?'

The daisies chimed in, 'Just wait for the sun!
We'll dance till we can't, oh, this marathon's fun!'
But the lilies rolled eyes, with dramatic flair,
Content to just lounge, not a worry or care.

Then came a wild breeze, tousled the scene,
With petals a-flying like confetti so keen.
All the flowers laughed, falling over in rows,
"What a spectacle!" croaked a wise old crow.

As night wrapped its arms round the garden's grand show,

The blossoms all chirped, 'We're the best, don't you know?'
For laughter and color, they spilled in the night,
As dreams danced around in the soft moonlight.

Echoes of the Earth

In the hills where the echoes bounce high and wide,
A worm told a joke, making hedgehogs collide.
'The grass is too ticklish, I swear on my shell!'
And the trees roared a laugh, 'Oh, do tell us well!'

The rocks rolled their eyes at the antics so grand,
While shadows danced lightly, just close at hand.
'The world is a stage, and we're all in the cast,'
Whispered the brook, with a splash and a blast.

A breeze carried whispers, 'Now isn't this fun?
Who knew dirt could giggle and nature could run?'
And a flower chimed in, 'I could dance all day!'
While the sun threw confetti, to brighten the play.

So next time you wander through forests and fields,
Remember the laughter that nature now yields.
For the ground is alive with secrets and glee,
Let your heart write the echoes, just wait and see!

Rhapsody of the Rose

In the garden, a rose got a jest,
Claiming the sun as its personal guest.
But the daisies laughed, oh so loud,
"You're just a poser, not royalty, shroud!"

With thorns like armor, it tried to prance,
Yet bees buzzed by with a cheeky glance.
"You're just a flower in a floral fight,
We prefer the bee's bumble – that's pure delight!"

The petals unfurled, a splash of hue,
"Knock knock! Who's there? It's pollen for you!"
The squirrels chuckled, rolling on ground,
As the rose's ego went round and round.

So here's to blossoms, bright and absurd,
Whispering tales that are wildly blurred.
For even in gardens, where beauty shines,
Laughter grows free, amidst tangled vines.

Sketches of Springtime

Springtime giggles in colors so bright,
With bunnies that hop in sheer delight.
The tulips wear hats, oh such a show,
While daffodils dance in a breezy flow.

A butterfly struts in polka dot flair,
Chasing a bee with a stylish air.
"Catch me if you can!" the buggy transmits,
The bee just buzzes, rolling its wits.

The grass blades gossip, tickling each toe,
"Why wear shoes? Let the bare feet glow!"
A picnic spread with sandwiches grand,
But ants march in lines – it's their quicksand!

With laughter like sunshine, warm from above,
Each bloom shares a joke, too sweet to shove.
Come join the merriment, let worries fling,
In this charming canvas, where all hearts sing.

Reflections of Radiance

Under the shade of a giggling tree,
A squirrel claimed, "The sky's calling me!"
With acorns for hats, it tried to fly,
But landed in leaves with a little sigh.

Daisies held court with a whimsical air,
Telling tall tales of their fragrant flair.
"We're the chosen, the crème de la crème,
While snobby roses just pose with a gem!"

Amidst the blooms, a potbellied frog,
Croaked out a sonnet, while lost in the fog.
"Ribbit, ribbit, dear friends, heed my tune,
Why sit on a leaf when you can dance under the moon?"

In this meadow of laughter, join the jest,
With giggles and blooms, it's simply the best.
For every petal wears a tale bright,
And chuckles are born in nature's delight.

Verses Amidst the Verdure

Among tall ferns, a monkey swings wide,
Bringing the jungle to laughter's side.
With one silly leap, it tickles a leaf,
Causing giggles that bring moments of relief.

The fronds all chatter, sharing their puns,
While the sun winks down, warming the runs.
"Why was the fern not invited to play?
Because it missed the zest of the sunny buffet!"

Where blooms sprout voices, in waves they dance,
Wishing each critter a chance for romance.
Yet the daisies roll eyes, 'it's quite the show,
Who knew the green could be such a pro?'

So here's to the verdant, the lush, and the green,
Bringing laughter where none have been seen.
With whimsy that sprouts, just give it a whirl,
For fun in the foliage is surely the pearl!

Harmonics of the Horizons

In the garden, a gnome plays a tune,
His hat is too big, his dance makes us swoon.
The sunflowers sway, with giggles they share,
While bees buzz around in a whimsical flair.

The carrots debate who's the best in the stew,
While zucchini insists that he's trendy and new.
A cucumber winks and says, "Look at me shine!"
The veggies all laugh, "You're a little too fine!"

A scarecrow complains about crows stealing crumbs,
While his pants start to dance, and everyone hums.
In this patch of delight, their joy is contagious,
Even the worms find the rhythm outrageous!

So gather your friends for this uproarious ride,
In the world of the green, where silliness hides.
With laughter and whimsy, let spirits be free,
The garden's a stage, come and join the jubilee!

The Grail of Green

In the realm of the leaves, where mischief abounds,
A broccoli knight fights with jest in the grounds.
His armor is tasty, a salad delight,
Yet peas keep on giggling—I'm ready to bite!

A quest for a treasure, a tomato so bold,
They say it's the ripest, a sight to behold.
But the onions all cry, "Oh, who's that to date?"
It's just a plain fruit with a jelly-filled fate!

Now carrots get jealous, they start to defend,
"Are we not the crunchies? Where's our shining end?"
The lettuce rolls eyes, whispers, "Don't take the bait,
For the grand joke is on us—we're the salad plate!"

Yet through all the banter, there's laughter galore,
As friends share their tales, ever hungry for more.
In laughter and munching, their stories entwine,
For humor's the treasure that's simply divine!

Parables of the Petal Path

On a journey of blooms, where mischief does bloom,
A daisy declares, "I'll bring joy to this gloom!"
While roses all gossip, their thorns tucked away,
"Did you hear about Tulip? She danced all day!"

The violets giggle, asking, "What's so funny?"
"Why do bees buzz? Because flowers are honey!"
A sunflower winks, surveying the scene,
"Join my comedy club—it's quite plant-astic, you'll glean!"

Each petal a story, each leaf holds a jest,
With blossom and banter, they spring at their best.
A gathering merry, with laughter that swells,
In the gardens of giggles, where every tale dwells!

So skip down the path, let joy be your guide,
In this patch of delight, where humor can't hide.
For nature's own laughter is simply a breeze,
Join the playful parade, and be sure to tease!

Tales from the Tulips

In a field of bright tulips, a mischief they weave,
Where the wind tells the stories, and all of them grieve.
"Why bloom in the shade?" one petal exclaimed,
"Let's dance in the sun!" and the others just claimed.

The bees hold a meeting, they're buzzing with glee,
"Let's paint the whole garden! Just us, can't you see?"
They gather their colors, a rainbow on the rise,
While butterflies roll their eyes with surprise.

"Why do the dandelions never wear suits?"
A tulip inquired with odd little hoots.
"Because they're too wild!" came a snicker, a shout,
"They'd rather just scatter, not destined to sprout!"

So laughter and florals, they mix in a swirl,
In the uproarious stories where silliness twirls.
From the daffodils' quips to the roses' sweet sighs,
In the realm of the blooms, let the funny arise!

Mystical Minutes in the Garden

In a patch of weeds, a frog took a seat,
He told a tall tale, oh what a treat!
With a wink and a hop, he shared his grand quest,
To find the best bug, he's surely the best!

A sunflower danced, with a grin on its face,
Claiming it's faster than a fast-paced race.
The leaves all chuckled, they couldn't agree,
"For the slowest of blooms, you're quite the speedy!"

A dandelion wore a fanciful crown,
Proclaiming, "I'm here to take over the town!"
The daisies just giggled, they knew it was fluff,
"In the kingdom of weeds, you're simply too tough!"

So in this strange patch, with laughter and cheer,
Time melts in the sun, and worries disappear.
With whispers of joy from the grass to the skies,
Nature's own jesters, where humor lies.

The Bloom of Lore

In the garden's embrace, a gnome spun a yarn,
Of flowers with secrets, both silly and grand.
A rose with a blush, said it's shy and coy,
But behind all that beauty, it's just a big toy!

Lilies debated which dress they would wear,
While tulips in ribbons combed through their hair.
One claimed the finest, with glamour and flair,
The other just sighed, "You're grasping at air!"

A lilac complained about that pesky bee,
"I swear he just buzzes to bother me!"
But a nearby daffodil chuckled and said,
"Buzzing is easy, try laughing instead!"

The crocus chimed in, "This springtime is grand,
Let's host a big party, let's all join hand!"
As petals all twirled in a jovial jest,
In the bloom of their lore, they felt truly blessed.

Memories in the Mist

Through the morning fog, a clamorous chant,
A batch of old mushrooms that liked to recant.
"Remember that time we played hide and seek?"
"I hid in plain sight, and I wasn't so sleek!"

A misty old willow swayed gently and sighed,
"Dear friends, oh how quickly we laughed and we cried.
With the dew on our caps, we danced 'til it glowed,
And shared silly tales of our mushroom abode!"

The ferns whispered secrets of sunrises past,
Of shadowy dances, that fit them quite fast.
"Let's weave a new story, right here in the haze,
With chuckles and joy, let's brighten our days!"

As the mist gently faded, so did their cares,
In each hug of the air, they shed all their snares.
With laughter entwined, they basked in the bliss,
Creating sweet memories, sealed with a kiss.

Stories Wrapped in Green

In a leafy retreat, where the sunlight drips,
A stocky old mushroom told tales with his quips.
Of squirrels on bikes and a snail with a hat,
He spoke of wild rides that just made them laugh!

A vine stretched its arms, said it would enthrall,
With stories of plants that could hear when you call.
"Just the other day, I heard a grill shout,
'What's cooking, good looking?' the flowers all sprouted!"

So the daisies conspired with the roses so red,
To prank the tall thistle, they hatched quite a thread.
They dressed up a bee in a costume so wild,
But when it took flight, it buzzed and it smiled!

As the sun dipped below and night took its stage,
The garden kept laughing, unfolding each page.
With stories in green and humor galore,
In nature's great book, there's always more!

The Flowered Folio

In a garden where daisies dance high,
A squirrel wore sunglasses, oh my!
He tried to impress a blue butterfly,
But tripped on a tulip and began to cry.

The roses were gossiping, oh what a scene,
About a tulip who thought she was queen.
Her crown was a daisy, quite small and mean,
Winning the title? Just a beautiful dream.

A bee with a bowtie buzzed through the bunch,
Claiming he'd break the world record for lunch.
He feasted on nectar, just after a crunch,
But dropped all his snacks; guess he lost that hunch.

With friends all around, laughter spread wide,
In a garden of gigs, not a frown to hide.
Each flower unique, let their quirks collide,
Finding joy in the chaos, let fun be our guide.

The Ode of Orchids

Orchids in the corner, all strutting their stuff,
In vibrant attire, they're really quite tough.
One tried telling jokes, but they were too rough,
Still, the crowd giggled, saying, "That's just enough!"

A cactus named Spike wore a hat on his head,
Claiming he'd blossom; all the others just fled.
"Too prickly for friendship!" the sunflowers said,
But they laughed it off, not a tear to shed.

The violets conspired, a prank on the way,
They swapped all the pollen; it caused quite a sway.
The bees danced confused, that's how they played,
In a world full of blooms, no one's ever dismayed.

Under the moonlight, they shared all their dreams,
About elixirs and magic, or so it seems.
With humor and blooms, laughter bustles and beams,
In the garden's embrace, we bloom in our themes.

Legends in Lavender

In fields of lavender, tales start to sprout,
A gnome with a beard was dancing about.
He tripped on a sprout, causing quite a rout,
All the flowers giggled, oh what a clout!

A bee with a vision, wanted to create,
The sweetest of nectar, a sugary fate.
But he lost his way and decided to skate,
Ended in clover, now isn't that great?

The sunlight was clever; it played every game,
Chasing the shadows, igniting the flame.
The daisies all cheered, calling out his name,
In laughter and light, nothing ever the same.

The twilight was comical, laughter did ignite,
In a world where silliness took joyous flight.
With each fragrant breeze, everything felt right,
Legends in laughter, a colorful sight.

Songs of the Saffron

Saffron's a singer, with tunes oh so bright,
He croons to the daisies by morning's first light.
But he sings off key—what a dreadful sight,
Yet all join in, for the joy feels just right.

A sunflower named Ray brought a joke to the crowd,
"Why did the berry sing so loud?"
The garlic chuckled, "It's very proud!
But be careful of ketchup; it's just too loud!"

A nightingale perched, joined in the fun,
Trying his best, with a laugh and a pun.
But instead of a song, it was more like a run,
As the insects erupted in giggles, well done!

Every flower gathered, let mischief unfold,
With humor and laughter, they cherished the gold.
Through songs and sweet whimsy, the world they behold,
In gardens alive, every moment retold.

www.ingramcontent.com/pod-product-compliance
Lightning Source LLC
Chambersburg PA
CBHW072223070526
44585CB00015B/1459